# FLOURISHING SHADOWS
# SOMBRAS FLORECIENTES

Camino del Sol

*A Latinx Literary Series*

Rigoberto González, Series Editor

JUAN FELIPE HERRERA
TRANSLATED BY LAURO FLORES

# FLOURISHING SHADOWS
# SOMBRAS FLORECIENTES

## A Chicano Howl

THE UNIVERSITY OF
ARIZONA PRESS
TUCSON

The University of Arizona Press
www.uapress.arizona.edu

We respectfully acknowledge the University of Arizona is on the land and territories of Indigenous peoples. Today, Arizona is home to twenty-two federally recognized tribes, with Tucson being home to the O'odham and the Yaqui. The university strives to build sustainable relationships with sovereign Native Nations and Indigenous communities through education offerings, partnerships, and community service.



ISBN-13: 978-0-8165-5701-1 (paperback)
ISBN-13: 978-0-8165-5702-8 (ebook)

Cover design by Leigh McDonald
Cover art by Juan Felipe Herrera
Designed and typeset by Leigh McDonald in Calluna 10.5/14, Payson WF, and Irby WF (display)
Interior art by Juan Felipe Herrera: Chinese Bamboo Brush, India ink on Bristol White 100lb paper, with tracing natural textured paper pressed.

Publication of this book is made possible in part by the proceeds of a permanent endowment created with the assistance of a Challenge Grant from the National Endowment for the Humanities, a federal agency.

Library of Congress Cataloging-in-Publication Data
Names: Herrera, Juan Felipe author | Flores, Lauro, 1950– translator
Title: Flourishing shadows : Sombras florecientes : a Chicano howl / Juan Felipe Herrera ; translated by Lauro Flores.
Other titles: Sombras florecientes | Camino del sol
Description: Tucson : University of Arizona Press, 2026. | Series: Camino del sol : a Latinx literary series | In English and Spanish.
Identifiers: LCCN 2026008414 (print) | LCCN 2026008415 (ebook) | ISBN 9780816557011 paperback | ISBN 9780816557028 ebook
Subjects: LCGFT: Poetry
Classification: LCC PS3558.E74 F58 2026 (print) | LCC PS3558.E74 (ebook)
LC record available at https://lccn.loc.gov/2026008414
LC ebook record available at https://lccn.loc.gov/2026008415

Printed in the United States of America
♾ This paper meets the requirements of ANSI/NISO Z39.48-1992 (Permanence of Paper).

# CONTENTS / ÍNDICE

# FOREWORD

## A Chicano Howl

These are challenging times. As we begin the second quarter of the twenty-first century, the sociopolitical landscape of the United States is marked by a shift toward a hardened brand of conservatism. Hatred, intolerance, and xenophobia are now openly the order of the day. The leaders and proponents of this drive continue to stir the emotions, and actions, of the populace by harping on issues that often target the most vulnerable groups. Prominent among these matters are of course immigration and the Mexican border. The demonization of the "invading horde of barbarians" that pose a threat to national integrity has become exacerbated and is now ubiquitous.

At its core, this book by Juan Felipe Herrera is a critique of the current state of affairs, an exploration of the ways in which *ideology*, in the Lukácsian sense of this term, operates and is manipulated by the main actors in this drama (farce?) through their performances at rallies, political events, and other forms of mass gatherings. The final objective of the "Nonreality Machine" they have set in motion, the poet seems to suggest, is to hypnotize and condition the audience, thereby turning them into believers, followers, and unconditional supporters. To this end, they use a series of base elements coming from religion, psychology, and mere fantasy—for example, attributing messianic or divine powers to the leader. In the same vein, a reiterative speech, the insistent repetition of key words and slogans, contributes greatly to produce the intended mesmerizing effect. In this regard, it is interesting to note Herrera's use of anaphora throughout this poem—a rhetorical device he has displayed in other works. On one hand, it seems to function here as a parody of the language pattern employed by politicians and other demagogues to agitate the masses and compel them to rally behind their ideological program. On the other hand, it can also be interpreted as a statement, as a practical example, of how the same devices can be used to counter the hegemonic discourse espoused by the reactionary forces.

Other, seemingly more subtle features, such the "crimson ties," the red "speaking caps," and the coded language of certain bodily gestures, "hand symbols for violent times," are also vital cogs in the mechanism.

More than a critique, this book can be regarded as the poet's response to the urgency of the situation. With his distinctive style and lyrical resourcefulness, Herrera is calling on us to reflect on the commonalities of our collective human condition and seek alternative voices: voices that express new ideas, ideas of kindness, care, and compassion, not anger and cruelty. His, of course, is one of those soothing, sensible voices. It always has been. "Migrants"—he has said—"are human beings, true families in search of happiness, food, clothes, a secure environment for survival, and employment in a land that is in part historically theirs."

Yet *Flourishing Shadows* is not a manifesto. Herrera's assessment of the current, distorted controversy around immigration leads him organically into the realm of the autobiographical—a thematic element that has been recurrent in many of his texts. Thus, he makes seamless connections with his family's migratory experience, his early travels and contact with Indigenous communities in southern Mexico, and the pivotal years he spent in San Francisco surrounded by friends and fellow artists, many of whom have passed away already.

His father, Emilio, "jumped a train . . . / from . . . Chihuahua / and made it to Denver, Colorado, when it was snowing"; his mother, Lucha Quintana, and her sisters "took a train from Tepito [Mexico City] / and arrived at Customs at the Juárez Borderline." His uncles Jeno, Beto, and Chente Quintana "signed up for the army / at Fort Bliss." They were all part of the legion of "shadows," those migrants who have left their homes and arrived in the United States (in "America"), especially in the Southwest, a land that was once part of Mexico, in search of a better life.

In 1970, as an undergraduate student at the University of California, Los Angeles, with the support of a grant from that institution's Chicano Studies Research Center, Herrera visited three Indigenous communities in Mexico—the Totonac peoples in Tabasco, the Huichol in Nayarit, and the Lacandón Maya in Chiapas. Those experiences have left a strong imprint on him and have become a narrative line in many of his works—*Mayan Drifter* (1997), for example, and this one.

After graduating with a BA from UCLA, Herrera joined the graduate program in anthropology at Stanford University. His proposed dissertation project was intended to be an ethnography of San Francisco's Latino poetry, its history and landscape. As things turned out, that project didn't come to fruition, for better or worse. Nevertheless, as a longtime resident of San Francisco, he himself became an integral part of that landscape. Herrera's references and at times detailed description of the locations of the apartments where he, his mother, and some of his close friends lived—the streets, cafés, and other places that were their "stomping grounds"—not only make this book, at least in part, a veritable topography of San Francisco but also underscore its autobiographical dimension.

Juan Felipe's recognition of his own place within the poetic tradition of San Francisco can be detected in the homage he pays to the Beat poets, especially Allen Ginsberg. His references to "America" and "Howl," two of Ginsberg's iconic poems—both in *"Howl" and Other Poems* (1956)—are obvious. At one point, Herrera's poetic persona says (yells), "I am howling / can you hear me America," and, in general, his conversation with a personified *America* regarding the treatment of immigrants clearly mimics Ginsberg's reproaches to the country for its politics, militarism, paranoia, and the complicitous role of the mass media in those affairs. In the same vein, the irregular structure in *Flourishing Shadows*, the seemingly spontaneous, free-form quality of the stanzas, endows the poem with an oral quality suggesting that the composition is designed to be performed, to be heard, rather than read. For me, a most significant aspect of all this lies in the "conversation" that Herrera sustains not only with America but also with Ginsberg and the Beat generation—that is, the appropriation of the discourse by a most unexpected voice: the voice of a Chicano, a child of immigrants, the offspring of a people who continue to be marginalized and vilified. A group that remains in the shadows despite their many contributions to the betterment of the United States of *America*. His lines "I notice the best minds of this generation / & the elders rethinking the New, creating," echo the first line of Ginsberg's "Howl": "I saw the best minds of my generation destroyed by madness, starving hysterical naked."

Juan Felipe Herrera speaks on behalf of the underdog, especially the immigrants, those *flourishing shadows* that wander through the pages of his book. For many, this makes him an *engagé* writer. The dictionaries define *engagé* as an "artist morally committed to a particular aim or cause." Over the last fifty years, Herrera has been a champion for the weak and vulnerable and a steadfast advocate of using art to promote global peace, harmony, and human understanding for the sake of our collective survival.

*Lauro Flores*
University of Washington, Seattle
December 31, 2024

# PREFACIO

## Un aullido chicano

El momento actual es un período de enormes desafíos. Al inicio del segundo cuarto del siglo XXI, el panorama sociopolítico de los Estados Unidos está marcado por un radical giro hacia un conservadurismo endurecido. El odio, la intolerancia y la xenofobia están a la orden del día. Los líderes y demás proponentes de este giro agitan sistemáticamente las emociones, y también las acciones, del populacho al enfocar sus comentarios, de manera machacona, en temas que impactan a los grupos más vulnerables de la población. En particular, las polémicas en torno a la inmigración y la frontera con México destacan dentro de este contexto. La satanización de "la horda de invasores bárbaros" que amenazan la integridad nacional se ha exacerbado y es ahora un tópico común.

En su meollo, este libro de Juan Felipe Herrera es una crítica de la situación actual, una exploración de la forma en que la *ideología*, en el sentido lukácsiano del término, opera y es manipulada por los actores principales de este drama (¿farsa?) a través del papel que desempeñan en los mítines, manifestaciones y demás eventos políticos. El principal objetivo de esa "Máquina de Irrealidad" que han puesto en marcha, como parece sugerir Herrera, es hipnotizar al público convirtiéndolo así en un ejército de seguidores fieles, de adeptos acríticos e incondicionales. Con este fin, utilizan una serie de elementos básicos derivados de la religión, de la psicología y, en última instancia, de la mera fantasía—por ejemplo, el hecho de asignarle atributos mesiánicos o divinos al líder. Del mismo modo, el empleo de un lenguaje reiterativo, la repetición machacona de ciertas frases y palabras clave, contribuye en gran medida a lograr el efecto deseado: mesmerizar del público. En este sentido, resulta interesante notar el uso que hace Herrera de la anáfora en este poema—un recurso retórico que ha utilizado ya en otras de sus obras—. Por un lado, se puede alegar que ello es una parodia del patrón retórico que utilizan los políticos y demás demagogos para agitar a las masas y, como ya he dicho antes, obligarlas así a acatar su agenda ideológica. Por otra parte, esto mismo se puede interpretar como una suerte de declaración de fe, es decir como un ejemplo práctico de cómo es posible echar mano de los mismos recursos, las mismas armas, para desafiar y contrarrestar el discurso hegemónico.

Otros elementos aparentemente más sutiles, tales como las "corbatas carmesíes", las rojas "gorras parlanchinas" y el lenguaje codificado de ciertos símbolos y gestos corporales, "señales de mano", "símbolos de mano para tiempos violentos", también son parte vital del mismo engranaje.

Más que una crítica como tal, este libro puede ser visto como la respuesta del poeta ante la urgencia de la situación. Con su ingenio lírico y distintivo estilo, Herrera nos está instando a reflexionar sobre nuestras semejanzas, sobre nuestra común condición humana, y a buscar voces alternativas, voces que expresen nuevas ideas, ideas de amabilidad, compasión y cariño, no de ira y crueldad. La suya es, por supuesto, una de esas voces razonables, apacibles y generosas. Siempre lo ha sido. Entre otras cosas, ha dicho, "Los migrantes son seres humanos, auténticas familias en busca de felicidad, alimento, ropa, un entorno seguro para su supervivencia y empleo en una tierra que, en parte, es históricamente suya".

No obstante, *Sombras florecientes* no es un manifiesto. La evaluación que hace Herrera de la actual y distorsionada controversia en torno al tema de la inmigración lo conduce orgánicamente al terreno de lo autobiográfico—un hilo temático que ha sido recurrente en muchos de sus textos—. De tal manera, elabora unas conexiones fluidas con la historia migratoria de su familia, sus tempranos viajes y experiencias con las comunidades indígenas de México, y las esenciales memorias de los años que vivió en San Francisco, California, rodeado de amigos y compañeros artistas, muchos de los cuales ya han muerto.

Su padre, Emilio, "salt[ó] a un tren, sin boleto . . . / [desde] Chihuahua / y lleg[ó] a Denver, Colorado, cuando nevaba"; su madre, Lucha Quintana, y sus tías "tomaron el tren desde Tepito / y arribaron a la Aduana en la frontera de Juárez"; sus tíos Jeno, Beto y Chente Quintana "se alistaron en el ejército / en el Fuerte Bliss". Todos ellos forman parte de esa legión de "sombras", de esos migrantes que han dejado atrás sus hogares para llegar a los Estados Unidos (a "América"), en particular al Suroeste, territorio que una vez fue parte de México, en busca de oportunidades y una vida mejor.

En 1970, cuando era alumno subgraduado en la Universidad de California, Los Angeles, y con el apoyo de una beca que le otorgó el Centro de Investigaciones de Estudios Chicanos de dicha institución, Herrera viajó a México y tuvo la oportunidad de visitar tres comunidades indígenas: los totonacas en Tabasco, los huicholes en la sierra de Nayarit, y los mayas lacandones en Chiapas. Tales experiencias han dejado una huella profunda en él, y se han convertido en un hilo temático presente en muchos de sus textos—como en *Mayan Drifter* (1997), por ejemplo, y en éste, *Sombras florecientes*.

Una vez concluidos sus estudios en UCLA, Herrera ingresó al programa de posgrado del departamento de antropología en la Universidad de Stanford. Allí anticipaba elaborar su disertación a partir de un estudio etnográfico de la historia y el panorama poético latino de San Francisco. Para bien o para mal, el plan no prosperó. Sin embargo, su residencia en aquella ciudad por un tiempo considerable lo convirtió en una parte integral de dicho panorama. Las múltiples referencias y frecuentes descripciones detalladas que hace Herrera acerca de la ubicación de los apartamentos donde vivían él, su madre y algunos de sus amigos cercanos, los nombres de las calles, los cafés y demás sitios que frecuentaban hacen de este libro, al menos en parte, una auténtica topografía de San Francisco, y a la vez subrayan su dimensión autobiográfica.

La conciencia de Juan Felipe acerca del lugar que ocupa dentro del marco de la tradición poética de San Francisco se advierte en el homenaje que les rinde a los poetas Beat, en particular a Allen Ginsberg. Sus referencias a "America" y "Howl" (Aullido), los dos poemas más icónicos del autor, ambos publicados en el volumen *"Howl" and Other Poems* (1956), son obvias. En un verso de *Sombras*, el hablante lírico de Herrera dice (grita), "Estoy aullando / ¿puedes oírme, América?" y, en general, su conversación, su alegato con una América personificada acerca del maltrato de los inmigrantes indiscutiblemente imita los reproches que Ginsberg le hiciera antes a este país a causa de su política, su militarismo, su paranoia y la complicidad de los medios de comunicación en tales menesteres. Del mismo modo, la estructura irregular de *Sombras florecientes*, la aparente espontaneidad de las estrofas y el verso libre le imprimen a la composición una calidad de oralidad que sugiere, como ocurre en el caso de Ginsberg, que el poema está diseñado para ser oído, como *performance*, no para ser leído. Para mí, un aspecto significativo es la "conversación" que Herrera sostiene no solo con esa América personificada, sino con el mismo Ginsberg y la generación Beat—es decir, la apropiación del discurso por parte de una voz inesperada: la voz de un chicano, un hijo de inmigrantes que forma parte de un pueblo que sigue siendo marginalizado y vilipendiado—. Un grupo que ha permanecido en las sombras a pesar de sus múltiples aportes al progreso y bienestar de este país, de los Estados Unidos de *América*. Sus palabras "Noto las mejores mentes de esta generación / & los mayores repensando lo Nuevo, creando" también son eco del primer verso de "Howl", el poema emblemático de Ginsberg: "He visto las mejores mentes de mi generación destruidas por la locura, hambrientas histéricas desnudas".

Juan Felipe Herrera habla por los de abajo, por los inmigrantes, en particular, esas *sombras florecientes* que deambulan por las páginas de su libro. Para algunos, esto lo convierte en un escritor comprometido (*un écrivain engagé*). Los diccionarios definen *engagé* como un "artista moralmente comprometido con una meta o una causa particular". Durante los últimos cincuenta años, Herrera ha sido un firme defensor de los desvalidos, y siempre ha abogado por poner el arte al servicio de la paz, la armonía y la comprensión humana. De ello depende nuestra supervivencia colectiva.

*Lauro Flores*
University of Washington, Seattle
31 de diciembre de 2024

# ACKNOWLEDGMENTS AND NOTES

In 1970, while studying at the University of California, Los Angeles, I set out on a voyage to three Indigenous zones in Mexico. I was concerned with the survival and daily life of the Totonac native peoples of Veracruz and Villahermosa—in particular, the ceremony of El Palo Volador, celebrated annually in Tuxpan, Veracruz. I met a Totonac family, four young men and sons of Señor Severo Martínez, maestro. This took place within the larger arena of the fiestas of Tuxpan.

I also visited the last of the Lacandón Maya peoples in their villages and lands in Chiapas—Najá and Lacanja Chan Sayab. Lastly, I visited the Huichol communities in the outskirts of Tepic, Nayarit, and later in the village in the Sierra del Nayar where they lived, El Colorín. I invited friends from UCLA—Manuel, Lin, and Tomás. In this book, I include a number of "advisors" and deities: Tauyepá (Father Sun), Tatewarí (Grandfather Fire), and Tutú (Messenger Hummingbird). Also, I mention the muvieri (healing wand) and Kauyumari (Blue Deer), advisor to the shaman, Maraákame.

I thank Ramón Medina Silva and his partner, Lupe de la Cruz Ríos, and the people of their village, El Colorín, on the tip of the sierra. I thank all the Huichol of the sierras of Nayarit—about 30,000 today. I thank Pepe Chambor from the Lacandón Maya village of Lacanja Chan Sayab and Kayúm Ma'ax and family from Najá. And elder Chan K'in, RIP. I thank Gertrude Blom, founder of Casa Na Bolom, the Lacandón Maya cultural center in San Cristóbal de las Casas, Chiapas, as well as the voladores from Villahermosa.

While at UCLA, I wrote a proposal to the Chicano Studies Research Center regarding travel to three areas of culturally endangered Indigenous peoples in Mexico: the Totonaca, the Lacandón Maya, and the Huichol. The Huichol make annual pilgrimages across Mexico—some to the USA.

I thank my professors, Barbara Myerhoff (RIP), Peter Furst, Renato Rosaldo, and George Collier (RIP), who pointed the way for me. And I thank the board of the UCLA Chicano Studies Research Center in 1970: Ray Castro, Roberto Sifuentes, Juan Gómez-Quiñones, and Moctesuma Esparza.

Many appreciations to Dr. Lauro Flores from the University of Washington, Seattle, for his advice and the Spanish translation of this collection.

For the Poetry Foundation, Chicago. For the MacArthur Foundation, for your kind and generous support. For Fresno State. For Joe Castro and familia. For Saúl Jiménez Sandoval and familia. For Fresno and the San Joaquín Valley, for Valley Children's Hospital. For all my students and dear friends. For the University of California, Riverside.

For all my lovely familias. Thank you. Tom Lutz and Laurie. For all my publishers; for my book agents, Kendra Marcus, Minju Chang; and my lecture agents, Blue Flower Arts. All my appreciations and love.

*Juan Felipe Herrera*
Fresno, California
December 21, 2024

# RECONOCIMIENTOS Y NOTAS

En 1970, cuando yo era alumno en la Universidad de California, Los Angeles, emprendí un viaje a tres zonas indígenas de México. Me interesaba la supervivencia y la vida cotidiana de los pueblos totonacas nativos de Veracruz y Villahermosa—en particular, la ceremonia del Palo Volador que se celebra anualmente en Tuxpan, Veracruz. Allí conocí a una familia totonaca con cuatro jóvenes, hijos del Sr. Severo Martínez, maestro. Esto ocurrió dentro del marco más amplio de la celebración de las fiestas de Tuxpan.

También visité a los últimos mayas lacandones en sus aldeas y tierras, en Chiapas—Najá y Lacanja Chan Sayab. Por último, visité a las comunidades huicholes en las afueras de Tepic, Nayarit, y más tarde en la Sierra del Nayar, en la localidad de El Colorín, en donde ellos vivían. Invité a algunos amigos de UCLA—Manuel, Lin y Tomás. En este libro incluyo a una serie de "asesores" y deidades: Tauyepá (Padre Sol), Tatewarí (Abuelo Fuego) y Tutú (Colibrí Mensajero). También menciono el "muvieri", la varita curativa, y Kauyumari, Venado Azul, asesor del chamán, Maraákame.

Les doy las gracias a Ramón Medina Silva y su compañera, Lupe de la Cruz Ríos, y a la gente de El Colorín, en la cumbre de la sierra. Mi agradecimiento a todos los huicholes de las sierras de Nayarit, quienes suman unos 30,000 hoy día. Las gracias a Pepe Chambor de la aldea lacandona Lacanja Chan Sayab, a Kayúm Maax y familia de Najá, y al anciano Chan K'in, QEPD. Muchas gracias también a Gertrude Blom, fundadora de Casa Na Bolom, el centro cultural lacandón de San Cristóbal de Las Casas, Chiapas, y a los voladores de Villahermosa.

En UCLA sometí una propuesta al Centro de Investigaciones de Estudios Chicanos solicitando apoyo para visitar esas tres regiones culturales indígenas en peligro de extinción en México: la totonaca, la lacandona y la huichol. Los huicholes realizan peregrinajes anuales por todo México, y a veces en los Estados Unidos.

Quiero darles las gracias a mis maestros, Barbara Myerhoff (QEPD), Peter Furst, Renato Rosaldo y George Collier (QEPD), quienes me señalaron el camino a seguir. Y gracias también a la mesa directiva del Centro de Investigaciones de Estudios Chicanos de UCLA en 1970: Ray Castro, Roberto Sifuentes, Juan Gómez-Quiñones y Moctesuma Esparza.

Mi profundo aprecio al Dr. Lauro Flores de la Universidad de Washington, Seattle, por su consejo y la traducción de este volumen.

Para la Poetry Foundation, Chicago. Para la Fundación MacArthur, por su amable y generoso apoyo. Para Fresno State. Para Joe Castro y familia. Para Saúl Jiménez Sandoval y familia. Para Fresno y el Valle de San Joaquín, para el Valley Children's Hospital. Para todos mis alumnos y queridos amigos. Para la Universidad de California, Riverside.

Para todas mis hermosas familias. Gracias. Tom Lutz y Laurie. Para todos mis editores; para mis agentes literarios, Kendra Marcus, Minju Chang; y mis agentes de conferencias, Blue Flower Arts. Todo mi aprecio y cariño.

*Juan Felipe Herrera*
Fresno, California
21 de diciembre de 2024

*Flourishing Shadows*

*For my parents, Lucha Quintana and Felipe Emilio Herrera, Rest in Love*

*for all Migrants, Immigrants, Humanity, Earth*
*for all those who did not survive, for all migrant youth and their teachers*

*for all my dear friends, poets and artists, through the years, this is for you*
*for Pedro Ortiz Vásquez, for many who have passed on, RIP*
*for Alfredo Arreguín, RIP, and his partner of many years, Susie*

*for Margo, my familias, children and grandchildren*
*for my teachers, students, professors, and*
*for all the poets of the world and lovers of the earth and its peoples*
*for all the singers of Mexico and Latin America*
*for all Native communities*

*for my uncles, Jeno, Beto, Chente, Fernando*
*for my tías, Alvina, Teresa, Lela, who migrated in the early 1900s*
*who did their best to survive in the big city*

*for my mother, Lucha, my father, Felipe, who did their best in the fields,*
*roadsides, small towns, El Paso, TX, and barrio Logan Heights*
*for all the Laureate Labbers, Fresno State.*

*For Anthony Cody; for Mai Der and Maxxy.*

*For you, Amalia, Karen, and Bob Alvarez*
*for all of those who have invited me to share poems*
*thru so many years, love. For Rob, Catalina, Katherine, and Anya at the Library*
*of Congress. For all my teatristas since 1967.*

I dedicate these poems to all migrants of our borderlands and of the world.

We were never illegal; we were labeled illegal.

*Hartos de andar, seguimos creciendo bajo el sol*
*Tired of walking, we keep flourishing under the sun*

—AFTER MERCEDES SOSA

*I came home to live the way*
*Life should always be*

—JACK HIRSCHMAN

I

# FLOURISHING SHADOWS

I notice the best minds of this generation
& the elders rethinking the New, creating
may we follow their meditations

I notice the políticos & the legislators & their crimson ties
may their minds be cleansed & humble

I notice the rallies of ideological hypnosis
I notice the forced unreality machine
crashing our truth
all the lies & the hand symbols for violent times

our minds will not be held captive
as Czesław Miłosz said against Hitlerism in the '40s

& against Stalinism

I notice the repetition of contaminating jingles &
oscillating performances on the carousel of erasure
& violent solidarity

will we crumble aghast as the desire for insurrection
and hunger for mass deportations rumble toward us

I am calling the thawing winds
I am calling the southwesters as Frost walked the last trails
Will we join the rain dance will we kneel and recite
the G# of the buried dreams of every beaten flower

will we dismantle the forced Nonreality Machine
calls for the Mass Deportations

will you salute the choking walls it brings
raise the squirming guns again
call the armed guards again & razor wire fences again

Grandmother Última Grande with cane & wheelchair
                    treads the waters
                              leads the thousands
                                        from Oaxaca & Huehuetitlán
                                           from Tegucigalpa

from Panamá
from Tapachula
& San Cristóbal & Talismán
                              from Ixcuintla

from Pachuca
& Tijuana, La Obrera & Calexico & La Nada
to these borderlands on fire

Screaming border walls fall now
screaming dead rise up from el río Grande

I notice the ripped Galaxy on their spine
I notice the fire spirals I notice
the moon & its 500 Blue Deer advisors Kauyumari
descend from the pueblos El Picacho & El Colorín
so we dance under the ice lights and read we read
the spark nights of Tatetwarí Grandfather Fire
now we stand on Sierra del Nayar
the circle of elder drummers of the Azteca Tepo
we gather with our elders
once again the women dance & shuffle under the moon

there is harmony
once again there is unity
once again there is kindness
once again we are One

*tired of walking under the sun we still flourish*

Tutú, Hummingbird, send us your messages
across sky and through cloud hats on mountains & sing
& dissolve on our sombreros & pantalones & rebozos

*you are infinite* Tutú says
*we are all life* elders chant

Ramón Medina Silva & Lupe de la Cruz Ríos
our last healers raise the hawk feathers
wrapped in estambre yarn & a filed point of the muvieri
they bow to the young one on the solar ground
they heal him
they brush across his chest
they pull the inner thorns of illness
from his heart from his belly

we shall walk out healed
aware
we shall create our metropolis Ciudad Quetzal Libre
we shall build on the other side
briars and brambles bushes & snakes
empty raw thorn scraped ranch acres
you must notice these empty lands

Our lands. Our hands. Your lands
our stolen lands of 1848

II

# LAND

We run we shout we see things dissolve
it is our land i
notice the bones vibrate
i notice the eyes still melting
there shall be no Mass Deportations we
sleep on stones
die under broken trees

*lost lost again* the desert ants whisper
*lost again you you*
they click into our midnight ears

lissen again sister brother

on these forbidden lands
we shall build Chinampas floating gardens

mud and seed rough-cut corn from our woven satchels
again we shall build again the pyramids of Moon and Sun
again we shall climb the red-orange steps to Venus
again we shall listen to her dawn blessings breathing
a new present of timelessness
an unknown happiness comes
an unknown starving limping with cut feet
we shall receive her instructions to continue

stop now
let us listen to Tutú Hummingbird's messages
we shall smear our faces on her fiery turquoise breast of canto
we shall scribble her poems in Xochitl in Cuicatl song

on our arms and cheeks the deer,
the sun, the ocean, the mountain, the Corn Dove Girl,
our Mother, Tatei Werika Wimari,
we carry her to the tiny Kaliway,

temple of branches & stones by the edge of the sierra
we shall bring offerings of frijol & maize & chicken blood
the healing muvieri wands of the hawk

*worn by walking under the sun still we flourish*
we will carry the jade-colored lake stones from Huehuetitlán
we will cross through Tapachula & Talismán at the end
of Chiapas & beginning of Guatemala
we will survive the Sahel of Africa
we shall cut through the last burned forests of Brazil
You will bow to the Jaguar of Argentina's green green jungles

we shall count the night fireflies of El Salvador on our crown
we shall shuffle through mud and cross sharp gravel
2,000 miles to begin

2,000 offerings to offer on the road
2,000 walls at every step at every generation
i notice the best minds of America
stolen and crushed with razor wire at the line

notice them stolen in America
notice them hypnotized
notice them captured & injected with lies
replaced with bullet casings
cast upon the endless flames

we will burn the psychic carpet
as it repeats its for-war designs & patterns of hate
as it bristles across time & the polished tables
of hopelessness of all our suffering
as we march from the South
barefoot carrying grandmother
and daughter and grandfather

from the world from the stars we breathe
again together again with determination again with
healing leaves in grandmother pouches we stop at the edge
of the Rio Grande we lift the bodies of María & Dulce
gone now the body of Javi in the cell on fire and
thousands marching in front of me behind me we
continue

do not think we are invisible we are
the brilliant minds living creating a brave new way
the world system is our system the galaxies are
our breath here now here now we almost have arrived
there will be no mass deportations
*tired & hurting by walking we still flourish under el sol*

do not go
reach out & listen we will not be shackled
do not drink the blood in the rivers it is living still
warming still singing to the moon goddess

America are you listening
America invisible do not be
America listen to Francisco X. Alarcón
in flight he sings he bows he offers petals of oneness
to the Four Directions he sings

*Tahui*
    *Tahui*
                *Tahui*
                *Tahui*

He bows as he sings as he casts the petal song
the cancer took him we all know he wanted to live
he wanted one more week like Víctor Martínez
who drifts with the eagles and hawks and writes
in his notebook luminous in-between clouds
cancer too cancer took him and dropped his poems
on Capp Street apartment #10

Remember Amy Uyematsu America
do not forget Janice Mirikitani America
or QR Hand or José Montoya or Alfonsito
or Rodrigo or Esteban or
Juanishi or Yolanda or René
all the poets & painters singers of galaxies and peace

still writing still scribbling still shouting &
Jack Hirschman still calling out Mayakovsky
in the skies above Broadway & Columbus
still delivering *Poetry Flash* in the open mercados

America
we are all still here

can you hear me
i left 17th & Mission Street
i dream of the second floor above Pollo Loco
where my mother lived in apartment #5
we shall not be mass deported
the land sky oceans and lakes
clouds and deserts
rocks and river stone shells
and pelicans over Muni Pier
and Alcatraz

look at me look at us now
we were never invisible
*worn by walking under the sun we still flourish*

We were never alone fishing the piers
we were painting the new deep sky of Dalí
we are the jagged rock faces of Cadaqués
we still wear the pelt mysteries of the Jaguar and Ocelotl
As Borges peered at the trapped animals
on the other side of the cage

America
America
you are all that
all this all us everyone

todos todas
nosotros
nosotras

Take my hand America
step into the waters green and gray
2,000 miles we shall wander together
swim and rush
our face will be blue brown white
our legs will be scraped & bloated
our backs will be pocked and sliced
our feet shall swell and burst
some have arrived
some are still there
we will not leave or float or die or abandon
girl child left inside the cell floor with a volleyball

reaching the shore too late America
you arrived too late America
lissen to Tutú the Hummingbird Messenger

America we will not be mass deported
are you listening
*worn & hurt as we walk under the sun we still flourish*

we shall build you anew
a new rain anew

shall caress you a new wind shall take you
a pyramid will open from your belly
walk the steps to the pedestal of torches
notice the lands the city of a new Teotihuacán
here in our lands by the river of thousands
Chinampas shall move you and feed you

El Palo Volador shall unfurl
our flying flowering bodies
and you shall land into a new time
a new generation
a new pueblo and mountain
our lands will be rumbling
our lands our hands our hearts our lives

I will be drumming a tiny can
at the tip of El Palo Volador
drum & dance I notice the world I notice the Earth
I breathe all its hope
I exhale all its suffering

drum & dance & drum & dance drum & dance & drum & dance

drum & dance & drum & dance
drum & dance & drum & dance
drum & dance & drum & dance
drum & dance & drum & dance
drum & dance & drum & dance
drum & dance & drum & dance
drum & dance & drum & dance
drum & dance & drum & dance
drum & dance & drum & dance
drum & dance & drum & dance
drum & dance & drum & dance
drum & dance & drum & dance

drum & dance & drum & dance
drum & dance & drum & dance
drum & dance & drum & dance
drum & dance & drum & dance
drum & dance & drum & dance
drum & dance & drum & dance

drum & dance & drum & dance

drum & dance & drum & dance
drum & dance & drum & dance
drum & dance & drum & dance
drum & dance & drum & dance
drum & dance & drum & dance
drum & dance & drum & dance
drum & dance & drum & dance
drum & dance & drum & dance
drum & dance & drum & dance
drum & dance & drum & dance

drum & dance & drum & dance
drum & dance & drum & dance drum
& dance & drum & dance

We will not be mass deported
take a moment America
breathe in breathe out
notice your calm your inner peace

Wars across the earth
Wars at every corner
Wars across the border
War lines under your eyes
every day every way
revenge burns every second

America when are you going
to stop when are you going
to walk down Columbus Ave.
& up Mission & 24th
when are you going to hold our hands
and pull us across Laredo, Ciudad Juárez, San Ysidro
& Tecate & Tijuana

Wars are your language
Revenge is your culture
America it is not too late

open the gates
break down the walls
there is no border
you were hallucinating

it was our bodies and our hands
reaching toward sun & moon
waiting to receive sacred rains from Tláloc

Breathe peace breathe humanity breathe unity
America it is easier than you think

BBBBBBBBBBB
BBBBBBBBBBBBBBBBBB
BBBBBBBBBBBBBBBBBBBBBBBBBBBBBB
BBBBBBBBBBBBBBBBBBBBBBBBBBBBBBBBBBBBBB
BBBBBBBBBBBBBBBBBBBBBBBBBBBBBBBBBBBBBBBBBBBBBB
RRRRRRR RRRRRRRRRRRRRRRRRRRRRRRRRRRRRR
EEEEEEEEEEEEEEEEEEEEEEEEEEEEEEEEEEEEEEEEEEEEEEEEEEE
AAAAAAAAAAAAAAAAAAAAAAAAAAAAAAAAAAAAAAAAAAAAAAA
TTTTTTTTTTTTTTTTTTTTTTTTTTTTTTTTTTTTTTTTTTTTTTTTTTTT
HHHHHHHHHHHHHHHHHHHHHHHHHHHHHHHHHHHHHHHHHHHHHH
E
E
E
E
E
E
E
E
E
E
E
E
E
E
E
E

I am howling

can you hear me America
I am bowing can you see me

can you feel me
I am standing in front of you in Chinatown
I am leaving to the Muni Pier near Bay Street

I am on the last cable car
Tito Quintana pulls the levers and rings the bell

My arms are open in J-Town to the Fillmore
I am calling you out from Manilatown
You can catch me on the 14 Mission bus
I will wait on 20th
not far from the pawnshop
across the street from
the old El Capitan movie theater

where have you been America
I saw you throwing beer bottles into the bars on Harrison St.
I am walking with the caravan tearing our feet

One more thing America
Stop bothering us
Stop jailing the minds of the people
lies & conspiracies hand symbols & speaking caps
it is time to kneel America & drag on your knees
to St. Peter's & confess on York Street
next to La Victoria restaurant
my mother, Lucy, can lead you

America
how long do i need to say all this
it's been a while
since 1967

since the Vietnam War
since the yellow rain cast upon the Hmong
since Hiroshima
since i was lost in Venice on Rose Street

It's time you take down the walls
fences and funky patrol stops in the middle of nowhere
asking for papers asking for green cards & our soul
did you forget America are you a legal citizen
this is Indian land this is Mexican land
We are America We are all America

It is not that easy America
we still remember we still have the songs & stories
we know the trails it is not the Border
it is our land

America cross your legs and meditate
lissen to the sacred Tutú hummingbird of the Huichol
listen to Grandfather Fire Tatewarí
it is not the border
it is our sweat it is our river it is our howl

America remember Allen Ginsberg
he's walking up Polk St. to Columbus
he's walking toward you
he's wearing Jack Hirschman's red shirt
he's taking a photo with Ferlinghetti, Di Prima
& Bob Kaufman who is coughing & Corso
who is still laughing & Kerouac still throwing
his crushed football all the way to Market St.
& scribbling about the Dharma

Do not forget America
We will not be mass deported &
you will not be mass deported

*tired of walking we still flourish under the sun*

Let us breathe life
let us ring tiny cymbals with our fingers
let us play congas at Aquatic Park with
Jimmy Biala & Rosemary Cadena
let us be the cooks at Caffe Sport on Green Street
let me swag into Caffe Trieste and grab an Espresso
scribble on this baby blue notebook

take a long look through the windows America
it is raining again I am drenched we have arrived
we are inside
Víctor sits next to me, Bobby, Janice & Amy & Francisco
we are all here again we are goofing around in the penumbra
our old stomping grounds i am calling you

Breathe life
breathe all life
slide on our trench coats wet down Van Ness to J-Town

your forced-alternative reality machine is out of coins
your captive mind radar is smoking
your border patrol Jeeps are stuck waiting to park on Geary St.

America do you know about human beings
we are here
soon we will be picking grapes in the Valley
every drop of wine has a drop of our sweat & tears
every funky burger has the tomatoes and onions
we pick under the hydrogen sun

Breathe in
with the clouds breathe out with the rain

Stand up and open your arms America
howl to the sky let the thunder wake you

notice our new generations of Freedom call
singing singing the parables repeating the
Four Noble Truths with Kerouac & Karen Brodine &
Genny Lim the Mission District is not far it is the gateway
to liberación
that is all America
we didn't come here to suffer you in detention cells
we walked miles thousands to embrace Libertad
in our lands because we are Libertad

we didn't come here to suffer you

Do not let racism be the next America
do not let extremism
with all its rationales be the next America
do not let walls & censors & shackles & wired cages
& small & long guns be the next America

Remember: "Let us gather in a flourishing way"
Take the road of humanity
Take the road of Unity and Harmony
Take the path of loving nature & the only Earth
Take the road of kindness & compassion
Take the road of suffering & meet us all on that road

en route to you America
we flourish

Let us breathe together & live under Tauyepá
the giving sun of all
I notice a new generation
with a new America
on their shoulders
& to the left side of their chest

America i must ask you
what is a migrant my friend

let us sit & meet each other
trade words and stories
our stories will be your stories
the stories will be painted
with yearning, sacrifice, and loss
& how we saved each other
& how we left with a satchel
of young maize and hard tortillas
oranges, bananas, and tamales
and just maybe a bottle of water
old medicines and sage ointments and scarves
and just maybe Gamesa cookies
& a can of chocolate dust

Lissen to me, America

What is a migrant
what was our vision

our map
what did we leave behind

Lissen again

it was death it was blood on the walls
a rooster too a few chickens
a house with one room & a tin roof
you must sit down with us
you must wear grandmother's shawl
you must walk these miles
that never end

do not think you are in command
there is no command
there is just one choice
to bring your familia to a land
that once was theirs

to a home that is warm
to a room of kindness and laughter
and tears of happiness

*worn & hurt by walking walking walking*
*under the sun we still flourish*

Lissen to me, America

Come and sit
and let us chat & let us embrace the truth
of our lives &
let us be sisters & brothers
once again                    America

Do not be afraid of the new pyramid
come and we shall build it together
it is called the City of the Gods
it is an ancient pyramid of the Sun & Moon
it is all of us
when you reach its peak you will
see the universe spirals from all directions
you will stand on the stones carved
with the face of a deity on the opposite side
you will collect the stars broken off galaxies
with your arms open you will dance
we will dance together become each other
it is on the other side of the walls
it is on new lands abandoned
it was there all along

do
u
see
it
?

¿

^

do
u
sí
tú

Do not fear the Palo Volador
30 meters high
the sacred and ancient tree of the Totonaca
at the top a disk where you can stand
dance & bow & play a tiny drum
tied to your wrist
your new name shall be Águila Sagrada
Sacred Eagle
4 of us will tie our legs to the tree
then we will unfurl
stars and a new galaxy
to come
in spirals we shall flow

Do not distrust the Chinampa
the floating garden
it was created by our ancestors
it saved thousands and fed thousands
it is time you must come
we will plant many things
and many will find flowers, squash, beans
chiles and Maize & they will live forever

Let us begin again
we will begin again
life and breath
happiness and community
this land will be this land
listen

We will not be mass deported
there will be no mass deportations
it will be like this
it will be like this

like this
like this
it will be

like this
like this
it will be

after the walls crumble
the waters shall enter turquoise
there will be celebrations at every
stop of the long journey
every city & town will welcome us
every soldier will remember us
every soldier will notice us they will shout
Lucha,
            Lela, Judith, Rosa, Alejo
                              Beto, Vicente, Tito
            Lela, Judith, Rosa, Alejo
                              María, Beto, Vicente, Tito

they will recognize their grandmothers
grandfathers & cousins & brothers
fathers & sisters & you
there will be offerings at each tiny shrine
by the forests of Guatemala and mountains
of El Salvador & Honduras

when we arrive
you will greet us with tears
you will greet us as if we lived
500 lives together
this is when we shall be brothers
and sisters once again

There is so much I can say
there is only so much I can tell you
it is as if I was reading you a poem
as if I was howling a poem
as if I was walking with my mother
speaking a poem that was buried for years
under a flower patch in Vista, Tepito, or El Niño Perdido

battered by storms and patrols and boots
there is only so much I can tell you

there were so many of us
on the road so many of us
following each other on the caravan
telling stories in the frozen nights
trading hard bread rolls a flattened cigarette
there were so many of us
so many of us who disappeared

when we reached the line the bridge
the razor wires & the boiling cells of steel
the strange courts & strange judges
for a moment we were visible again
for a moment we huddled
in a detention center and played volleyball

we left home we left our tiny garden
we left our rooster, el Chito, our chickens
brothers & sisters the tree that was always there
since I was 5 we left our lives it wasn't easy
we became wanderers we became targets
there is nothing now
there is this now what is this now
some made it to Juárez
some to El Paso
Some jumped a train like my father
from El Mulato, a municipio of Ojinaga, Chihuahua
and made it to Denver, Colorado, when it was snowing
he had never seen snow
some signed up for the army
at Fort Bliss like my tíos
Jeno & Beto & Chente Quintana
some took a train from Tepito
and arrived at Customs at the Juárez Borderline
like my mother Lucha my grandmother Juana
and my tía Lela a picture was taken

dressed in black they left to live in Segundo Barrio
in El Paso mortar and sleep on bricks

do not weep America
*worn & hurt by walking under the sun we still flourish*

many were separated from their children
the mother in jeans had to turn back to nowhere
in the lost darkness and disappear
the father had to turn round and later
fall under a broken bush silent silent

we are here at the edge
I am here with 2,000

outside the great river
for a moment we can see
we can walk without our feet bursting
or a child drowning

lissen lissen to me America

let's sit and have a bowl of frijoles
when we get to Tucson or Mesquite
salsa, tortillas, and fried papas
we'll peel charred chiles from a roaster
we'll round the fire
and smell the ancient stinging fragrance
inviting us to eat

we will look at each other's faces
our eyes seeing everything
so much left behind
so many torn and filled with hope
our clothes wet

breathing deep
exhaling slow

is this America
America America America
it is time
a long time for freedom
a long time for humanity

we have arrived
we have arrived

there shall not be a mass deportation
happiness kindness and love
will come down upon us
we will kneel upon our earth
and thank all beings & stars & trees
rivers & mountains
clouds & rivers & lakes

i & i
you & you
we & we
us & us

thank + kneel
kneel + all
all + thank

earth = being

***  ***.  ***

*tired & hurt walking & walking we flourish under the sun*

we shall not be mass deported

*********. ***  *

now we breathe now we now breath now we
now we breathe now we now breath now
now we breathe now we now breath
now we breathe now we now
now we breathe now we
now we breathe now
now we breathe
now we
now

Freedom

we

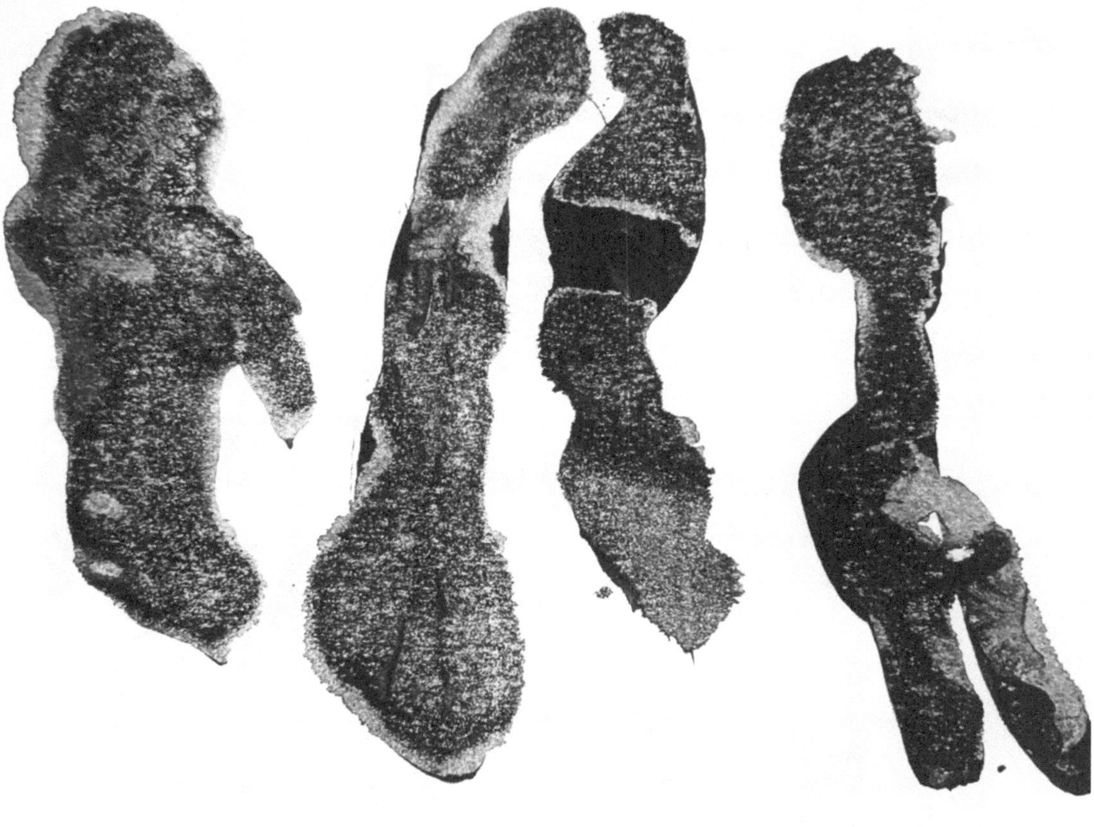

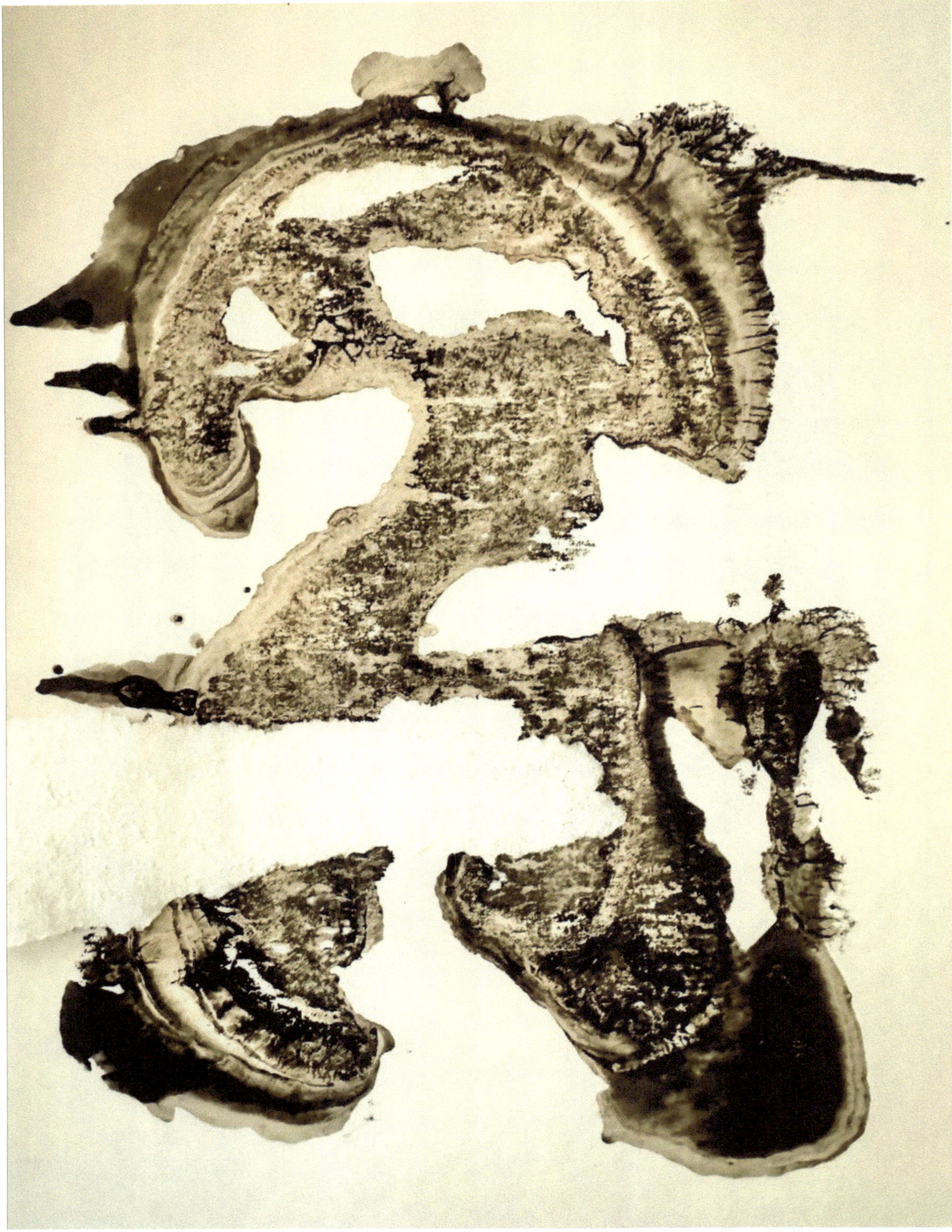

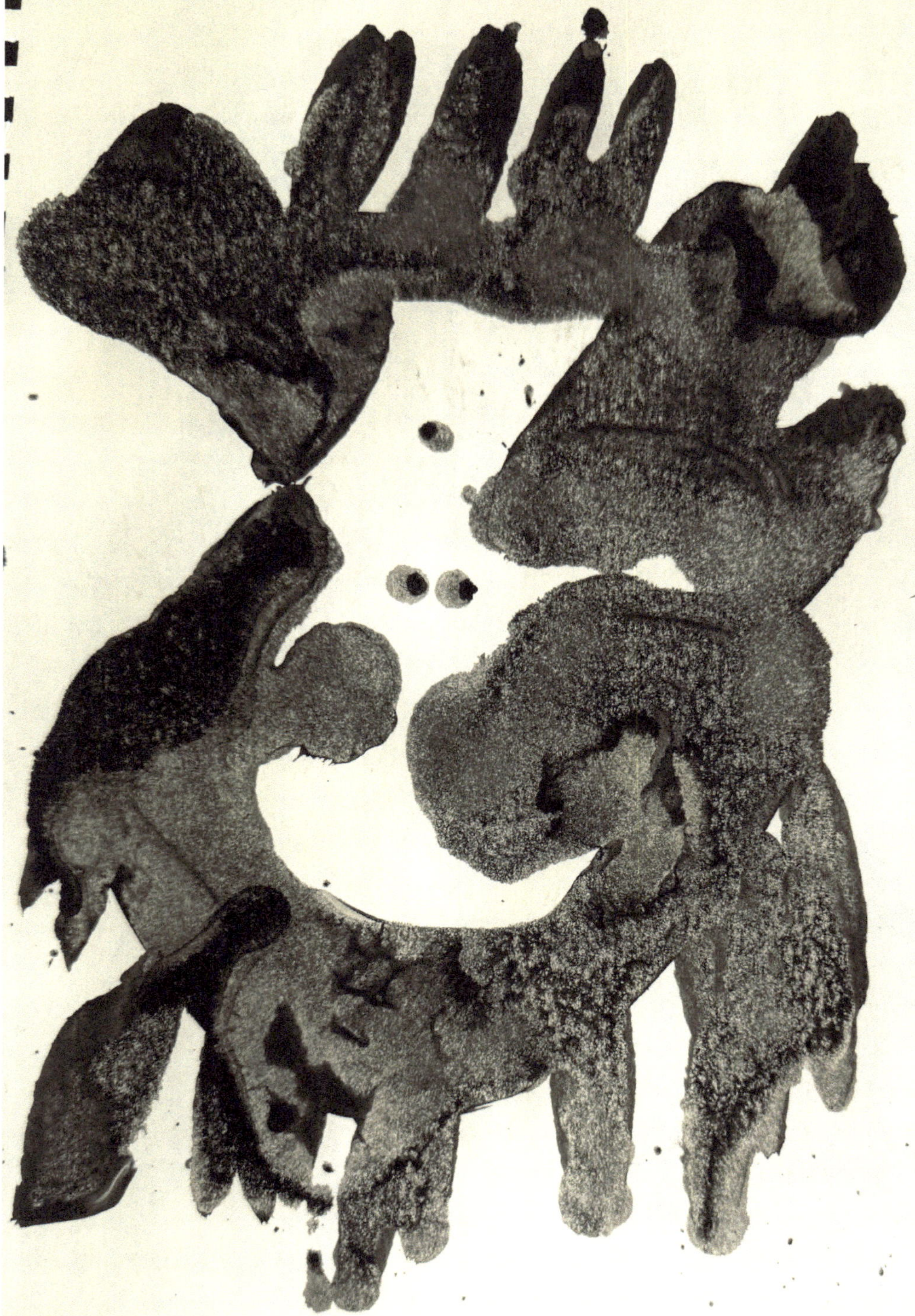

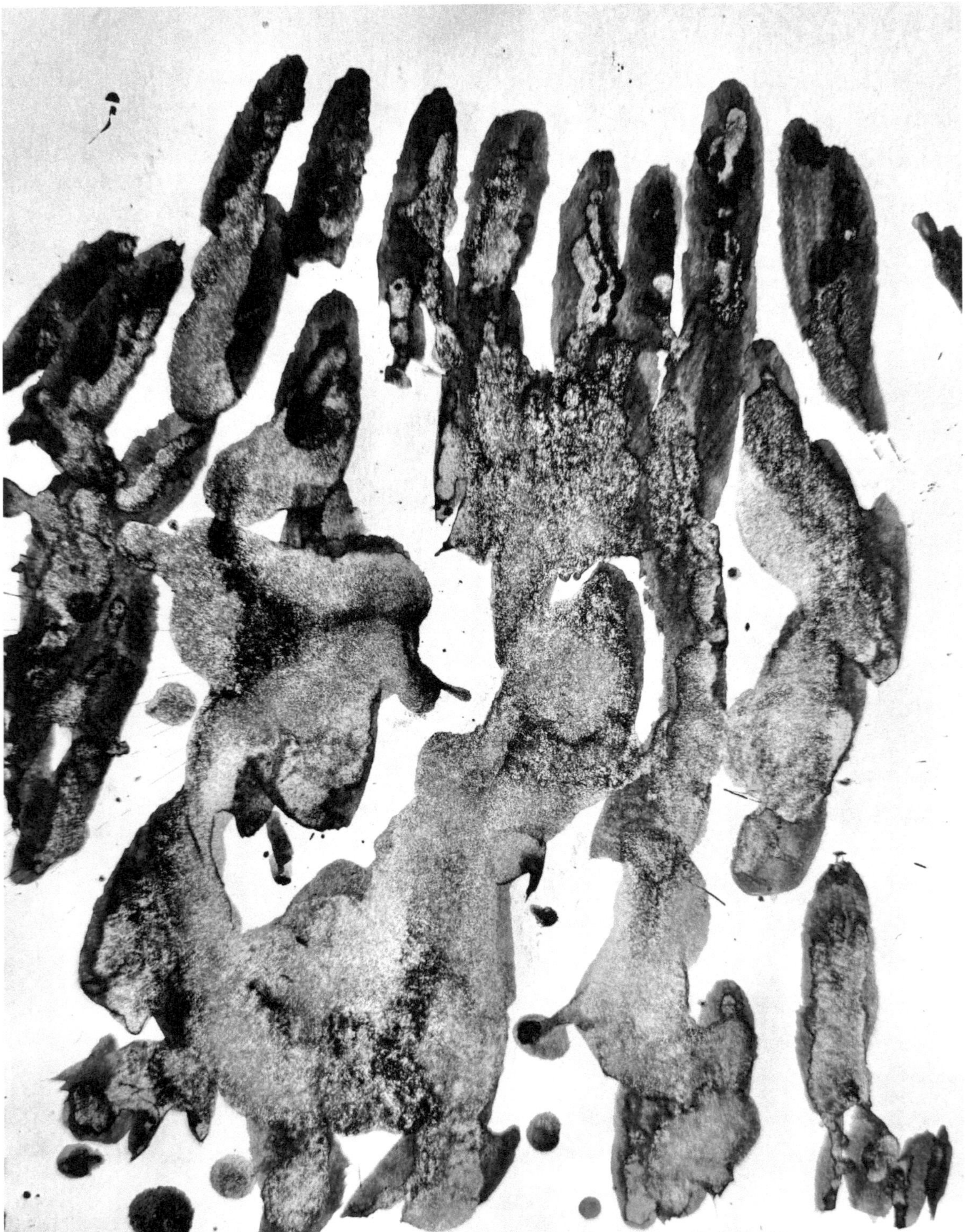

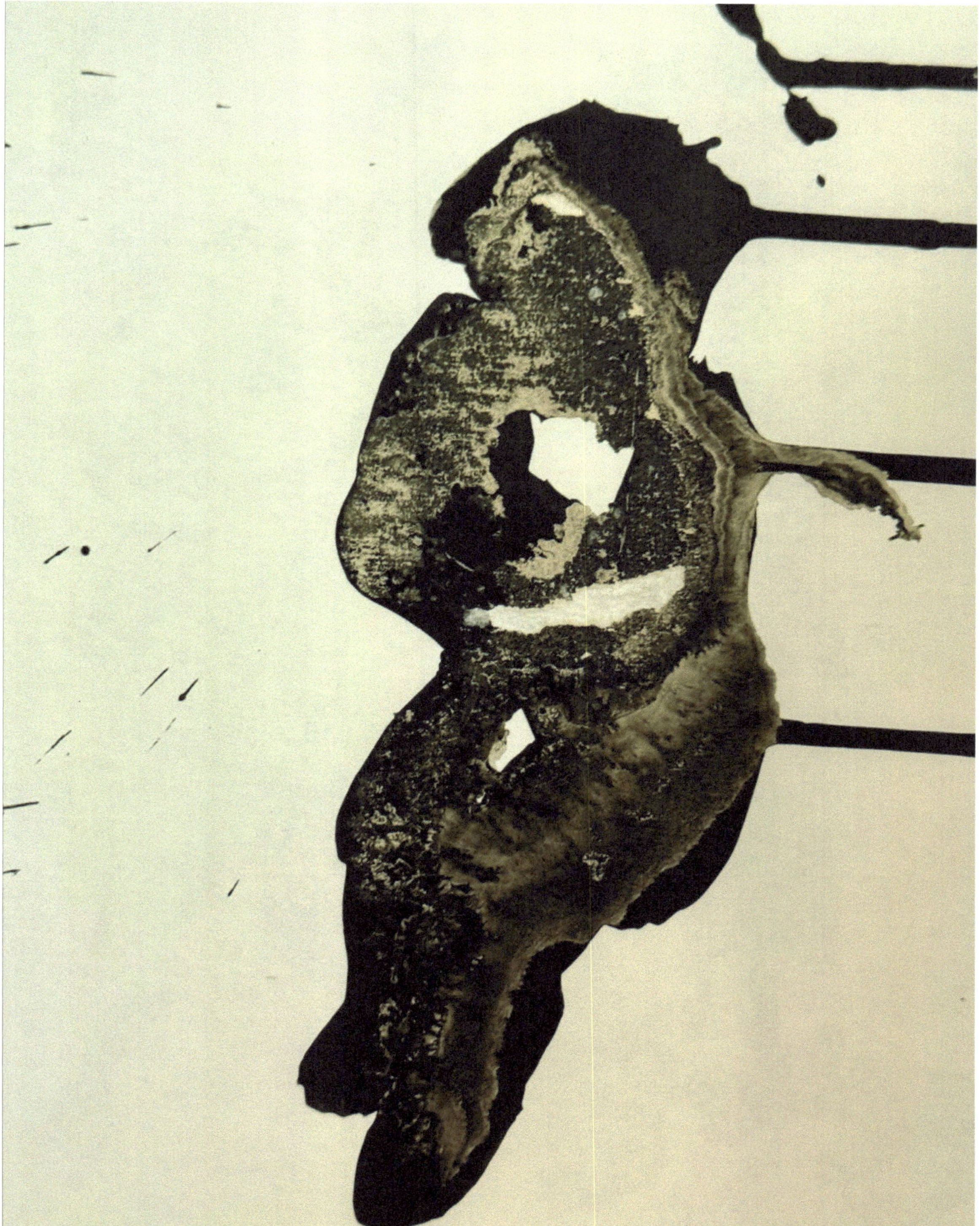

# *Sombras florecientes*

*Para mis padres, Lucha Quintana y Felipe Emilio Herrera, Descansen en Amor*

*para todos los Migrantes, Inmigrantes, la Humanidad, la Tierra*
*para todos aquellos que no sobrevivieron, para toda la juventud migrante y sus maestros*

*para todos mis queridos amigos, poetas y artistas, a través de los años, esto es para ustedes*
*para Pedro Ortiz Vásquez, para tantos que ya fallecieron, QEPD*
*para Alfredo Arreguín, QEPD, y su compañera de muchos años, Susie*

*para Margo, mis familias, hijos y nietos*
*para mis maestros, estudiantes, profesores y*
*para todos los poetas del mundo y los amantes de la tierra y su gente*
*para todos los cantantes de México y Latinoamérica*
*para todas las comunidades indígenas*

*para mis tíos, Jeno, Beto, Chente, Fernando*
*para mis tías, Alvina, Teresa, Lela, quienes migraron a principios de los años 1900*
*quienes hicieron su mejor esfuerzo para sobrevivir en la gran ciudad*

*para mi madre Lucha y mi padre Felipe, quienes se esforzaron en los campos agrícolas, en los bordes de los caminos, en los pueblos pequeños, en El Paso, TX y el barrio de Logan Heights*
*para todos los "Laureate Labbers" en Fresno State.*

*Para Anthony Cody; para Mai Der y Maxxy.*

*Para ustedes, Amalia, Karen y Bob Alvarez*
*para todos los que me han invitado a compartir poemas*
*a través de tantos años, amor. Para Rob, Catalina, Katherine y Anya en la Biblioteca del Congreso. Para todos mis teatristas desde 1967.*

Dedico estos poemas a todos los migrantes de nuestra zona fronteriza y del mundo.

Nunca fuimos ilegales; se nos ha clasificado como ilegales.

*Hartos de andar, seguimos creciendo bajo el sol*
*Tired of walking, we keep flourishing under the sun*

—PARÁFRASIS DE MERCEDES SOSA

*Llegué a casa para vivir de la manera*
*En que la vida debería ser siempre.*

—JACK HIRSCHMAN

I

# SOMBRAS FLORECIENTES

Noto las mejores mentes de esta generación
& los mayores repensando lo Nuevo, creando
que sigamos sus meditaciones

Noto a los polítikos & los legisladores & sus corbatas carmesíes
que sus mentes sean limpiadas & humildes

Noto las asambleas de hipnosis ideológica
noto la máquina que fuerza la irrealidad
aplastando nuestra verdad
todas las mentiras & los símbolos de mano para tiempos violentos

nuestras mentes no permanecerán cautivas
como dijo Czesław Miłosz contra el hitlerismo en los años 40

y contra el estalinismo

noto la repetición de las cancioncillas contaminantes &
actuaciones oscilantes en el carrusel de la supresión
& violenta solidaridad

nos desmoronaremos horrorizados acaso cuando el deseo de insurrección
y el hambre de deportaciones masivas vocifere contra nosotros

Estoy llamando a los vientos del deshielo
Estoy llamando al vendaval del suroeste como Frost recorrió los últimos senderos
Nos uniremos a la danza de la lluvia, nos arrodillaremos para recitar

la clave de sol de los sueños enterrados de toda flor golpeada
desmantelaremos acaso la forzada Máquina de Irrealidad
los llamados a las Deportaciones Masivas

saludarás las asfixiantes murallas que trae consigo
levanta los inquietos fusiles retorciéndose una vez más
llama a los guardias armados otra vez & cercos de alambre de navajas de nuevo

Abuela Última Grande con bastón & silla de ruedas
camina por las aguas sin hundirse
dirige a miles
de Oaxaca & Huehuetitlán
de Tegucigalpa
de Panamá
de Tapachula
& San Cristóbal & Talismán
de Ixcuintla
de Pachuca
& Tijuana, La Obrera & Calexico & La Nada
a estas tierras fronterizas en llamas

Los muros fronterizos que gritan ahora se derrumban
los muertos gritando se elevan del río Bravo

yo noto la rasgada Galaxia en su espinazo
noto las espirales de fuego noto
la luna & sus 500 venados azules consejeros Kauyumaris
descienden de los pueblos El Picacho & El Colorín
así que nosotros danzamos bajo las luces heladas y leemos, leemos
las noches chispeantes del Abuelo Fuego Tatetwarí
ahora estamos parados en la Sierra del Nayar
el círculo de ancianos tamboreros de la Tepo Azteca
nos reunimos con nuestros ancianos
una vez más las mujeres danzan & arrastran los pies bajo la luna

hay armonía
una vez más hay unidad
una vez más hay dulzura
una vez más somos Uno

cansados de andar bajo el sol aún florecemos

Tutú, Colibrí, envíanos tus mensajes
a través del cielo y los gorros de nubes en las montañas & canta
& disuélvete en nuestros sombreros & pantalones & rebozos

*sóis infinitos* dice Tutú
*todos somos vida* los ancianos cantan

Ramón Medina Silva & Lupe de la Cruz Ríos
nuestros últimos curanderos elevan las plumas de halcón
envueltas en hilos de estambre & la punta limada del muvieri
se inclinan ante el joven en el suelo solar
lo sanan
rozan suavemente el muvieri sobre su pecho
le arrancan las espinas internas de la enfermedad
del corazón del vientre

saldremos sanos
conscientes
crearemos nuestra metrópolis Ciudad Quetzal Libre
construiremos al otro lado
brezos y zarzales & serpientes
acres de ranchos vacíos arañados por las crudas espinas
debes notar estos terrenos baldíos

Nuestras tierras. Nuestras manos. Tus tierras
nuestras tierras robadas en 1848

II

# TIERRA

Corremos gritamos vemos las cosas disolverse
es nuestra tierra yo
noto que los huesos vibran
noto los ojos todavía derritiéndose
no habrá Deportaciones Masivas. Nosotros
dormimos sobre piedras
morimos bajo árboles rotos

*perdido perdido de nuevo* susurran las hormigas del desierto
*perdido otra vez tú tú*
cliquean en nuestros oídos de medianoche

escucha de nuevo hermana, hermano

en estas tierras vedadas
construiremos Chinampas, huertos flotantes

barro y semilla maíz áspero de nuestros morrales tejidos
de nuevo construiremos las pirámides de la Luna y del Sol
de nuevo subiremos los escalones rojo-naranja de Venus
de nuevo escucharemos sus bendiciones del amanecer respirando
un nuevo presente de atemporalidad
llega una alegría desconocida llega
un hambrienta desconocida cojeando con los pies cortados
recibiremos sus instrucciones para continuar

detente ahora
escuchemos los mensajes del Colibrí Tutú
untaremos nuestros rostros en su ardiente pecho turquesa de canto
garabatearemos sus poemas canto in Xochitl in Cuicatl

en nuestros brazos y mejillas el ciervo,
el sol, el océano, la montaña, la Niña Paloma del Maíz,
nuestra Madre, Tatei Werika Wimari
la llevamos al pequeño Kaliway,

templo de ramas & piedras al borde de la sierra
traeremos ofrendas de frijol & maíz & sangre de pollo
las varitas curativas muvieri del halcón

*gastados por caminar bajo el sol aún florecemos*
llevaremos las piedras del lago de color de jade de Huehuetitlán
pasaremos por Tapachula & Talismán al final
de Chiapas & principios de Guatemala
sobreviviremos el Sahel de África
cortaremos a través de los últimos bosques quemados del Brasil
Te inclinarás ante el Jaguar de las verdes verdes selvas de Argentina

contaremos las luciérnagas nocturnas de El Salvador en nuestra corona
marcharemos a través del barro y cruzaremos por la grava afilada
2,000 millas por comenzar

2,000 ofrendas para ofrecer por el camino
2,000 murallas a cada paso en cada generación
noto las mejores mentes de América
robadas y aplastadas con alambre de navajas en la línea

las noto robadas en América
las noto hipnotizadas
las noto capturadas & inyectadas con mentiras
reemplazadas por casquillos de bala
arrojadas sobre las infinitas llamas

quemaremos la alfombra psíquica
mientras repite sus designios de guerra & patrones de odio
mientras se eriza a través del tiempo y las pulidas mesas
de la desesperanza, de todo nuestro sufrimiento
mientras marchamos desde el Sur
descalzos cargando a la abuela
a la hija, al abuelo

desde el mundo, desde las estrellas respiramos
de nuevo juntos de nuevo con determinación de nuevo con
hojas curativas en bolsas medicinales de abuela nos detenemos al borde
del río Bravo levantamos los cuerpos de María & Dulce
ahora ausente el cuerpo de Javi en la celda en llamas y
miles marchando delante de mí detrás de mí
continuamos

no pienses que somos invisibles, somos
las mentes brillantes que viven y crean una nueva y valiente senda
el sistema mundial es nuestro sistema las galaxias son
nuestro aliento aquí ahora aquí ahora casi hemos llegado
no habrá deportaciones masivas
cansados & doloridos por tanto caminar florecemos bajo el sol

no te vayas
acércate & escucha, no seremos encadenados
no bebas la sangre en los ríos, aún sigue viva
calentándose aún, cantándole a la diosa luna

América, ¿estás oyendo?
América, invisible no seas
América, escucha a Francisco X. Alarcón
en vuelo canta, se inclina, ofrece pétalos de unidad
a las cuatro puntos cardinales canta

*Tahui*
        *Tahui*
                                        *Tahui*
                                        *Tahui*

Se inclina mientras canta mientras lanza el canto de los pétalos
el cáncer se lo llevó, todos sabemos que quería vivir
que quería una semana más, como Víctor Martínez
quien flota con las águilas y los halcones y escribe
en su cuaderno luminosos entre-nubes
el cáncer, también el cáncer se lo llevó y dejó caer sus poemas
sobre la calle Capp, apartamento #10

Recuerda a Amy Uyematsu, América
no olvides a Janice Mirikitani, América
ni a QR Hand ni a José Montoya ni a Alfonsito
ni a Rodrigo ni a Esteban ni
a Juanishi ni a Yolanda o René
todos los poetas y pintores cantores de galaxias y paz

todavía escribiendo todavía garabateando todavía gritando &
Jack Hirschman todavía convocando a Mayakovsky
en los cielos sobre la Broadway & Columbus
todavía entregando *Poetry Flash* en los mercados públicos

América
todos seguimos aún aquí

¿puedes oírme?
me marché de la 17th & Mission
sueño con el segundo piso, arriba del Pollo Loco,
donde vivía mi madre, en el apartamento #5
no seremos deportados en masa
la tierra, el cielo, los océanos y lagos
nubes y desiertos
rocas y conchas de piedra de río
y pelícanos sobre el muelle Muni
y Alcatraz

mírame, míranos ahora
nunca fuimos invisibles
*desgastados por caminar bajo el sol aún florecemos*

Nunca estuvimos solos pescando en los muelles
estábamos pintando el nuevo cielo profundo de Dalí
somos los rostros rocosos y dentados de Cadaqués
todavía llevamos puestos los misterios de la piel del Jaguar y el Tigre
Así como Borges miró con dificultad los animales atrapados
al otro lado de la jaula

América
América
tú eres todo eso
todo esto, todo nosotros, todos

todos todas
nosotros
nosotras

Toma mi mano, América
entra en las aguas verdes y grises
2,000 millas recorreremos juntos
nadar y correr
nuestra cara será azul café blanca
nuestras piernas estarán raspadas & hinchadas
nuestras espaldas perforadas y rebanadas
nuestros pies se hincharán y reventarán
algunos han llegado
algunos todavía están allí
nosotros no partiremos ni flotaremos ni moriremos ni dejaremos
a la niña abandonada en el piso de una celda con una pelota de voleibol

alcanzando la orilla demasiado tarde, América
llegaste demasiado tarde, América
escucha a Tutú, el Colibrí Mensajero

América, no seremos deportados en masa
¿estás oyendo?
*gastados & heridos al caminar bajo el sol aún florecemos*

te construiremos de nuevo
una nueva lluvia de nuevo

te acariciará un nuevo viento te llevará
una pirámide se abrirá desde tu vientre
sube por los peldaños hasta el pedestal de antorchas
nota las tierras, la ciudad de una nueva Teotihuacán
aquí en nuestras tierras junto al río de miles
las chinampas te moverán y te alimentarán

El Palo Volador desplegará
nuestros florecientes cuerpos voladores
y tú aterrizarás en un nuevo tiempo
una nueva generación
un nuevo pueblo y una nueva montaña
nuestras tierras estarán retumbando
nuestras tierras, nuestras manos, nuestros corazones, nuestras vidas

yo estaré tamborileando una pequeña lata
en la punta del Palo Volador
tambor & danza noto el mundo noto la Tierra
respiro toda su esperanza
exhalo todo su sufrimiento

tambor & danza & tambor & danza tambor & danza & tambor & danza

tambor & danza & tambor & danza
tambor & danza & tambor & danza
tambor & danza & tambor & danza
tambor & danza & tambor & danza
tambor & danza & tambor & danza
tambor & danza & tambor & danza
tambor & danza & tambor & danza
tambor & danza & tambor & danza
tambor & danza & tambor & danza
tambor & danza & tambor & danza
tambor & danza & tambor & danza
tambor & danza & tambor & danza

tambor & danza & tambor & danza
tambor & danza & tambor & danza
tambor & danza & tambor & danza
tambor & danza & tambor & danza
tambor & danza & tambor & danza
tambor & danza & tambor & danza

tambor & danza & tambor & danza

tambor & danza & tambor & danza
tambor & danza & tambor & danza
tambor & danza & tambor & danza
tambor & danza & tambor & danza
tambor & danza & tambor & danza
tambor & danza & tambor & danza
tambor & danza & tambor & danza
tambor & danza & tambor & danza
tambor & danza & tambor & danza
tambor & danza & tambor & danza

tambor & danza & tambor & danza
tambor & danza & tambor & danza tambor
& danza & tambor & danza

No seremos deportados en masa
tómate un momento, América
inhala, exhala
observa tu calma, tu paz interior

Guerras en toda la tierra
Guerras en cada rincón
Guerras al otro lado de la frontera
líneas de Guerra bajo tus ojos
todos los días de cualquier forma
la venganza arde a cada segundo

América, ¿cuándo vas
a parar? ¿cuándo vas
a caminar por la avenida Columbus
& a subir por la Mission & 24th?
cuándo vas a tomarnos de la mano
y a tirar de nosotros a través de Laredo, Ciudad Juárez, San Ysidro
& Tecate & Tijuana

Las guerras son tu lengua
La venganza es tu cultura
América, no es demasiado tarde

abre las puertas
demuele las murallas
no hay frontera
estabas alucinando

eran nuestros cuerpos y nuestras manos
extendiéndose hacia el sol y la luna
esperando recibir sagradas lluvias de Tláloc

Respira paz respira humanidad respira unidad
América, es más fácil de lo que piensas

RRRRRRRRRRR

RRRRRRRRRRRRRRRRR

RRRRRRRRRRRRRRRRRRRRRRRRRRRRRR

RRRRRRRRRRRRRRRRRRRRRRRRRRRRRRRRRRRRRRR

RRRRRRR RRRRRRRRRRRRRRRRRRRRRRRRRRRRRRRRRRRRRRR

EEEEEEEEEEEEEEEEEEEEEEEEEEEEEEEEEEEEEEEEEEEEEEE

SSSSSSSSSSSSSSSSSSSSSSSSSSSSSSSSSSSSSSSSSSSSSSSSSS

PPPPPPPPPPPPPPPPPPPPPPPPPPPPPPPPPPPPPPPPPPPPPPPP

IIIIIIIIIIIIIIIIIIIIIIIIIIIIIIIIIIIIIIIIIIIIIIIIIIIIIIIIIIIIIIIIIIIIIIIIIIII

RRRRRRRRRRRRRRRRRRRRRRRRRRRRRRRRRRRRRRRRRRRRR

A

A

A

A

A

A

A

A

A

A

A

A

A

A

A

Estoy aullando

¿puedes oírme, América?
me estoy inclinando ante ti ¿puedes verme?

¿puedes sentirme?
estoy parado frente a ti en Chinatown
me voy al muelle Muni, cerca de Bay Street

estoy en el último tranvía
Tito Quintana tira de las palancas y toca la campana

Mis brazos están abiertos en J-Town hasta el Fillmore
te estoy llamando desde Manilatown
Puedes encontrarme en el autobús #14 de la Mission
esperaré en la calle 20
no muy lejos de la casa de empeño
al cruzar la calle del
antiguo cine El Capitán

¿dónde has estado, América?
te vi arrojando botellas de cerveza a los bares de Harrison St.
voy caminando con la caravana, despedazando nuestros pies

Una cosa más, América
Deja de molestarnos
Deja ya de encarcelar la mente de la gente
mentiras & conspiraciones señales de mano & gorras parlanchinas
es hora de arrodillarte América & arrastrarte de rodillas
hasta St. Peter & confesarte en York Street
al lado del restaurante La Victoria
mi madre, Lucy, puede guiarte

América
¿cuánto tiempo tengo que decir todo esto?
ya ha pasado bastante tiempo
desde 1967

desde la guerra de Vietnam
desde la lluvia amarilla que cayó sobre los Hmong
desde Hiroshima
desde que me perdí en Venice, en la calle Rose

Ya es hora de que derribes las murallas
los cercos y las fétidas patrullas que nos detienen en medio de la nada
exigiendo papeles exigiendo tarjetas verdes & nuestra alma
¿ya lo olvidaste, América? ¿eres tú acaso un ciudadano legal?
esta es tierra indígena, ésta es tierra mexicana
Nosotros somos América. Todos somos América

No es tan fácil, América
nosotros aún recordamos, aún conservamos los cantos & historias
conocemos los senderos, no es la Frontera,
es nuestra tierra

América cruza las piernas y medita
escucha al sagrado colibrí Tutú de los huicholes
escucha al Abuelo Fuego Tatewarí
no es la frontera
es nuestro sudor, es nuestro río, es nuestro aullido

América recuerda a Allen Ginsberg
va caminando por la calle Polk hacia Columbus
va caminando hacia ti
lleva puesta la camisa roja de Jack Hirschman
se está tomando una foto con Ferlinghetti, di Prima
& Bob Kaufman quien está tosiendo & Corso
quien sigue riendo & Kerouac quien está lanzando
su balón de fútbol aplastado hasta la calle Market
& garabateando acerca del Dharma

No lo olvides América
No seremos deportados en masa &
tú no serás deportada en masa

*hartos de caminar seguimos floreciendo bajo el sol*

Respiremos vida
hagamos sonar diminutos platillos con los dedos
toquemos congas en el Parque Acuático con
Jimmy Biala & Rosemary Cadena
seamos los cocineros en el Caffe Sport en Green Street
déjame entrar con estilo en el Caffe Trieste y tomar un espresso
garabatear en este cuaderno azul celeste

echa un buen vistazo por las ventanas, América
está lloviendo otra vez, estoy empapado, ya llegamos
estamos dentro
Víctor se sienta junto a mí, Bobby, Janice & Amy & Francisco
estamos aquí de nuevo bromeando en la penumbra
nuestro viejo territorio, te estoy llamando

Respira vida
respira toda la vida
deslízate en nuestras gabardinas mojadas de Van Ness a J-Town

tu máquina de realidad alternativa forzada se ha quedado sin monedas
tu radar de mentes cautivas está echando humo
tus Jeeps de la patrulla fronteriza están atascados esperando para estacionarse en
  la calle Geary

América, ¿sabes algo sobre los seres humanos?
aquí estamos
pronto estaremos cosechando uvas en el Valle
cada gota de vino contiene una gota de nuestro sudor & lágrimas
cada fétida hamburguesa lleva los tomates y cebollas
que nosotros cosechamos bajo el sol de hidrógeno

Aspira
con las nubes, exhala con la lluvia

Levántate y abre los brazos, América

aúlla al cielo, deja que el trueno te despierte
nota nuestras nuevas generaciones del llamado a la Libertad
cantando cantando las parábolas repitiendo las
Cuatro Nobles Verdades con Kerouac & Karen Brodine &
Genny Lim el Distrito de la Misión no está lejos, es la puerta de entrada
a la liberación
eso es todo, América
no vinimos aquí a sufrirte en celdas de detención
caminamos millas miles para abrazar la Libertad
en nuestras tierras porque nosotros somos la Libertad

no vinimos aquí para sufrirte

No permitas que el racismo sea la próxima América
no dejes que el extremismo
con todos sus razonamientos sea la próxima América
No permitas que los muros & los censores & los grilletes & las jaulas de alambre
& las armas de fuego pequeñas & largas sean la próxima América

Recuerda: "Reunámonos en forma floreciente"
Toma el camino de la humanidad
Toma el camino de la Unidad y la Armonía
Toma el sendero de amar la naturaleza & la única Tierra
Toma el camino de la bondad & la compasión
Toma el camino del sufrimiento & encuéntranos a todos en ese camino

en camino hacia ti, América
florecemos

Respiremos juntos & vivamos bajo Tauyepá
el sol dador de todos
noto una nueva generación
con una nueva América
sobre los hombros
& al lado izquierdo de su pecho

América debo preguntarte
¿qué es un migrante, amiga mía?

sentémonos & conozcámonos
intercambiemos palabras e historias
nuestras historias serán tus historias
las historias serán pintadas
con anhelo, sacrificio y pérdida
& cómo nos salvamos uno a otro
& cómo partimos con un saco
de maíz tierno y tortillas duras
naranjas, plátanos y tamales
y quizá sólo una botella de agua
viejos medicamentos y ungüentos de salvia y bufandas
y quizá solo galletas Gamesa
& una lata de polvo de chocolate

Escúchame, América

¿Qué es un migrante?
¿cuál fue nuestra visión,

nuestro mapa?
¿qué dejamos atrás?

Escucha de nuevo

fue la muerte, fue sangre en las paredes
también un gallo, unos cuantos pollos
una casa de un solo cuarto y techo de hojalata
debes sentarte con nosotros
debes ponerte el chal de la abuela
debes andar estas millas
que nunca terminan

no creas que estás al mando
no hay mando
hay solo una opción
traer a tu familia a una tierra
que una vez fue suya

a un hogar que es cálido
a una habitación llena de dulzura y risas
y lágrimas de felicidad

*desgastados & heridos por caminar caminar caminar*
*bajo el sol aún florecemos*

Escúchame, América

Ven y siéntate
y conversemos & abracemos la verdad
de nuestras vidas &
seamos hermanas & hermanos
una vez más                América

No tengas miedo de la nueva pirámide
ven y la construiremos juntos
la llaman Ciudad de los Dioses
es una antigua pirámide del Sol y la Luna
es todos nosotros
cuando alcances su cima verás
las espirales del universo en todas direcciones
te pararás en las piedras labradas
con el rostro de una deidad en el lado opuesto
recogerás las estrellas desprendidas de las galaxias
con los brazos abiertos danzarás
danzaremos juntos convirtiéndonos uno en el otro
está al otro lado de los muros
está en las nuevas tierras abandonadas
estuvo allí todo el tiempo

¿
la

v
e
s
?

^

t
ú
sí
tú

No le temas al Palo Volador
30 metros de altura
el sagrado y antiguo árbol de los totonacas
en su cima un disco en el que te puedes parar
danzar & inclinar & tocar un pequeño tambor
atado a tu muñeca
tu nuevo nombre será Águila Sagrada
Sacred Eagle
4 de nosotros ataremos nuestras piernas al árbol
después desplegaremos
estrellas y una nueva galaxia
por venir
en espirales fluiremos

No desconfíes de la chinampa
el jardín flotante
fue creado por nuestros ancestros
salvó a miles y alimentó a miles
es hora, debes venir
plantaremos muchas cosas
y muchos encontrarán flores, calabazas, frijoles
chiles y maíz & vivirán para siempre

Empecemos de nuevo
empezaremos de nuevo
vida y aliento
felicidad y comunidad
esta tierra será esta tierra
escucha

No seremos deportados en masa
no habrá deportaciones masivas
así será
así será

así
así
será

así
así
será

después de que las murallas se desmoronen
las aguas entrarán en turquesa
habrá celebraciones en cada
parada del largo viaje
cada ciudad & pueblo nos dará la bienvenida
cada soldado nos recordará
cada soldado nos notará, todos gritarán
Lucha,
Lela, Judith, Rosa, Alejo
Beto, Vicente, Tito
Lela, Judith, Rosa, Alejo
María, Beto, Vicente, Tito

reconocerán a sus abuelas
abuelos & primos & hermanos
padres & hermanas & tú
habrá ofrendas en cada pequeña capilla
por los bosques de Guatemala y las montañas
de El Salvador & Honduras

cuando lleguemos
nos saludarás con lágrimas
nos saludarás como si hubiéramos vivido
500 vidas juntos
es entonces cuando seremos hermanos
y hermanas una vez más

Hay tanto que puedo decir
pero hay un límite en lo que puedo decirte
es como si estuviera leyéndote un poema
como si estuviera aullando un poema
como si estuviera caminando con mi madre
pronunciando un poema que estuvo enterrado por años
bajo un jardín de flores en Vista, Tepito o El Niño Perdido

maltrecho por tormentas y patrullas y botas
hay un límite en lo que puedo decirte

éramos tantos
en el camino, tantos de nosotros
siguiéndonos unos a otros en la caravana
contando historias en las noches heladas
intercambiando bollos de pan duro un cigarrillo aplastado
éramos tantos
tantos de nosotros que desaparecieron

cuando llegamos a la línea el puente
los alambres de púas & las hirvientes celdas de acero
los extraños juzgados & los extraños jueces
por un momento volvimos a ser visibles de nuevo
por un momento nos apiñamos
en un centro de detención y jugamos voleibol

dejamos atrás nuestro hogar, dejamos nuestro pequeño jardín
dejamos nuestro gallo, el Chito, nuestros pollos
hermanos & hermanas el árbol que siempre estuvo allí
desde que yo tenía 5 años, dejamos nuestras vidas, no fue fácil
nos convertimos en nómadas, nos convertimos en objetivos de tiro
ahora ya no hay nada
existe este ahora ¿qué es este ahora?
algunos llegaron a Juárez
algunos a El Paso
Algunos saltaron a un tren, sin boleto, como mi padre
oriundo de El Mulato, municipio de Ojinaga, Chihuahua
y llegaron a Denver, Colorado, cuando nevaba
él nunca había visto la nieve
algunos se alistaron en el ejército
en el Fuerte Bliss, como mis tíos
Jeno & Beto & Chente Quintana
otros tomaron el tren desde Tepito
y arribaron a la Aduana en la frontera de Juárez
como mi madre Lucha, mi abuela Juana
y mi tía Lela, les tomaron una foto

vestidas de negro, se fueron a vivir en el Segundo Barrio
en El Paso a dormir sobre ladrillos

no llores, América
*desgastados & heridos por tanto caminar bajo el sol aún florecemos*

muchos fueron separados de sus hijos
la madre en pantalones de mezclilla tuvo que regresar hacia la nada
en la oscuridad perdida y desaparecer
el padre tuvo que dar la vuelta para después
caer bajo un arbusto quebrado, silente, silente

estamos aquí al borde
estoy aquí con otros 2,000

fuera del gran río
por un momento podemos ver
podemos caminar sin que nuestros pies revienten
o se ahogue un niño

escúchame, escúchame, América

sentémonos y tomemos un plato de frijoles
cuando lleguemos a Tucson o a Mesquite
salsa, tortillas y papas fritas
pelaremos chiles chamuscados de un asador
rodearemos el fuego
y oleremos la antigua y picante fragancia
invitándonos a comer

nos miraremos el rostro unos a otros
nuestros ojos viéndolo todo
tanto quedó atrás
tantos desgarrados y llenos de esperanza
nuestra ropa mojada

respirando profundo
exhalando lentamente

¿es ésta América?
América América América
ya es hora
un largo tiempo para la libertad
un largo tiempo para la humanidad

hemos llegado
hemos llegado

no habrá deportación masiva
alegría amabilidad y amor
descenderán sobre nosotros
nos arrodillaremos sobre nuestra tierra
y les daremos las gracias a todos los seres & estrellas & árboles
ríos & montañas
nubes & ríos & lagos

yo & yo
tú & tú
nosotros & nosotros
nosotros & nosotros

agradecer + arrodillarse
arrodillados + todos
todos + gracias

tierra = ser

***     ***.     ***

*cansados & heridos andando & andando florecemos bajo el sol*

no seremos deportados en masa

*********. ***     *

ahora respiramos ahora respiramos ahora nosotros
ahora respiramos ahora respiramos ahora
ahora respiramos ahora ahora respiramos
ahora respiramos ahora ahora
ahora respiramos ahora nosotros
ahora respiramos ahora
ahora respiramos
ahora nosotros
ahora

Libertad

nosotros

# WRITING NOTE

My critique of current political ideology is concerned with the mixture of psychology, religion, and performance by the actors of such ideology who in many ways lean on hypnotizing, or "conditioning," the audience through rallies and such. This hypnosis, or "conditioning," is accomplished by anaphoric and repetitive speech, terms, names, attire, colors, labels, and hand and finger symbols for the audience, in particular via rally events that serve in many ways as *rites of passage*; this is to say that all these cultural performance acts, language, and gestures by the speakers condition their audience into converts, believers, followers regarding the content of the speech and presentation and presenter. For example, if the presenter says migrants are "invaders" in such a manner, the followers begin to feel and think and act as if it is true. The religious aspect takes effect when the audience begins to assign religious status to the speaker, such as calling him or her "the chosen one," "holy," or "gifted with a religious task." We must dismiss such performative conditioning, falsehoods, and hypnosis. We must look for speakers who express true kindness, care, compassion, and new ideas for the people, not anger, suffering, and cruelty. Migrants are human beings, true families in search of happiness, food, clothes, a secure environment for survival, and employment in a land that is in part historically theirs.

*Juan Felipe Herrera*
Fresno, California
December 21, 2024
With abundant gratitude and love and kindness for all. Muchas gracias.

# NOTA SOBRE LA ESCRITURA

Mi crítica de la actual ideología política está relacionada con la mezcla de psicología, religión y arte escénico (o *performance)* que emplean los actores de tal ideología, quienes se apoyan de muchas maneras en hipnotizar, o "condicionar", al público, en mítines y demás. Tal hipnosis, o "condicionamiento", es acompañada por un discurso anafórico, reiterativo, compuesto de palabras, nombres, prendas de vestir, colores, rótulos y gestos con las manos y los dedos dirigidos a la audiencia en ciertas reuniones de masas que operan como *ritos de iniciación*; es decir que todas esas actuaciones culturales, lenguaje y gestos con las manos de los oradores condicionan a los integrantes del público, transformándolos en conversos, creyentes y seguidores fieles del contenido de los discursos y presentaciones, y del presentador. Por ejemplo, si el presentador dice en cierta forma que los migrantes son "invasores", los seguidores empiezan a sentir, a pensar y a actuar como si ello fuera cierto. El aspecto religioso entra en vigor cuando la audiencia empieza a asignarle un estatus religioso al hablante, al líder, llamándole "el escogido" o "la escogida", "santo" o "dotado de una tarea religiosa". Debemos descartar tal condicionamiento performativo, tales falsedades e hipnosis. Tenemos que buscar oradores que expresen una auténtica bondad, cuidado y compasión, nuevas ideas para la gente, no ira, sufrimiento y crueldad. Los migrantes son seres humanos, auténticas familias en busca de felicidad, alimento, ropa, un entorno seguro para su supervivencia y empleo en una tierra que, en parte, es históricamente suya.

*Juan Felipe Herrera*
Fresno, California
21 de diciembre de 2024
Con abundante gratitud, amor y bondad para todos. Muchas gracias.

# ABOUT THE AUTHOR AND TRANSLATOR

**Juan Felipe Herrera** was born in 1948 to farmworker parents. Herrera is a graduate of the University of California, Los Angeles; Stanford University; and the University of Iowa Writers' Workshop. The author of more than thirty-five books in various genres, Herrera served as Poet Laureate of the United States from 2015 to 2017. Herrera has taught Chicano and Latin American studies at California State University, Fresno, and creative writing at the University of California, Riverside, and has held numerous visiting positions. He is a professor emeritus at the Department of Chicano and Latin American Studies, Fresno State University, and is the current coordinator for the Laureate Lab Visual Wordist Studio at the Fresno State Library.

**Lauro Flores** is a professor at the University of Washington. He is the author, editor, or translator of several publications, including the anthology *The Floating Borderlands*, winner of the American Book Award.

**Juan Felipe Herrera** nació en 1948 de padres trabajadores agrícolas migrantes. Es egresado de la Universidad de California, Los Ángeles; la Universidad de Stanford; y el Taller de Escritores de la Universidad de Iowa. Autor de más de treinta y cinco libros en varios géneros, Herrera se desempeñó como Poeta Laureado de los Estados Unidos de 2015 a 2017. Ha dictado cursos de estudios chicanos y latinoamericanos en la Universidad Estatal de Fresno, y clases de escritura creativa en la Universidad de California en Riverside. Además, ha ocupado numerosos cargos de profesor visitante. Actualmente, es profesor emérito en el Departamento de Estudios Chicanos y Latinoamericanos de la Universidad Estatal de Fresno, y coordinador del Laureate Lab Visual Wordist Studio en la biblioteca de esa misma institución.

**Lauro Flores** es catedrático en la Universidad de Washington. Es autor, editor y traductor de varias publicaciones, incluyendo la antología *The Floating Borderlands*, ganadora del American Book Award (Premio Americano del Libro).